A Guide to Potty Training

Caroline Young

Illustrated by Shelagh McNicholas

Design and additional illustrations by Ruth Russell

Edited by Felicity Brooks

Internet links

For further information about Usborne Parents' Guides
and to visit the websites recommended in this book, go to
www.usborne-quicklinks.com
Click on 'Parents' Guides' or type in the keywords 'potty training'.

Contents

Introduction

Most parents and carers are delighted to say goodbye to nappies. Even if you use super-absorbent, leak-proof, odour-controlling disposable nappies, changing them is one more job to do. You are probably looking forward to the day when your child is potty-trained; when they can take themselves to the potty or toilet and do what they need to do with little help from you.

But before you circle a start date for training on the calendar, there are several things to consider, especially how?, when? and where? As small children have minds, and bodies, very much of their own, they may just not be ready to work to your timetable.

Most children crawl at around nine months and walk at around a year, but it's much harder to pinpoint when they will be potty-trained. If you accept that all children are different and that you need to adapt what you do and when you do it to suit your own child, you're much more likely to succeed. The key is to be flexible and to expect the unexpected.

Independence, for a small child, comes one step at a time, and cannot be hurried.

The training process

Potty-training is just one of the many, many things a child needs to learn as they grow up, but it is one of the things parents get most worried about. This book guides you through the whole process from start to finish. It outlines the different approaches you could take, offers advice on staying positive, and helps you to overcome any problems and setbacks you might have.

It also takes your needs into account: potty-training can be hard work, and you need to find an approach that suits your own circumstances as well as your own child. Above all, this book looks at how you can work with your child to get him or her potty-trained with the minimum mess and stress possible.

Useful tip

For the record, the average age for a child to be potty-trained (in the day) is between two and a half and three years old.

When is the right time?

Life with a small child is busy, and most people find that it's easier to cope if they plan ahead a little. We generally prefer things to happen when it suits us, and without any unexpected problems, and this could be why potty-training can come as such a shock: it doesn't fit into an ordered way of life at all. It's a process that a child has to learn – and they have to be ready to learn it before they begin.

This book describes the signs that show when your child may be ready, and takes you through all the steps to prepare for the 'big day'. Before this point, hard as it may be, it's important to resist the urge to make potty-training fit in with your other plans. You may want to have your child nappy-free by the end of the year, but if they show no signs of being ready to use a potty by November, you could be setting yourselves up for spectacular failure if you try to potty-train them then.

When to train

• Very few children are potty-trained before they are 20 months old and many children are still wearing a nappy at night until they are three – and some for longer.

• Before these ages, don't worry about whether your child is or isn't trained yet (whatever family and friends may tell you).

While they are learning

Even when your child shows all the signs of being ready, they will probably still have many accidents while they are training. Learning to respond to their body's signals and managing their own toileting takes lots and lots of practice and is not something you can do for them, however much you might want to. This book shows how to deal with this tricky phase and how to stay as calm as you can while you do so.

Some children are more reluctant than others to say goodbye to nappies.

Be prepared

It may not sound very inviting, but it's a good idea to do a bit of thinking about potty-training before you start doing it. Experts agree that being well-prepared is very helpful, so this section of the book looks at some ways of getting ready to start potty-training, and helps ensure that, once you begin, you are more likely to succeed.

Before you begin

How children learn to know when they need to go to the toilet

Different approaches to potty-training, from today's experts and from earlier generations

Tips on how to stop worrying about what other people think, or what other children can do, and when

Guidance on how to handle potty-training, and what will work best for you and your child

Control of when and where to wee and poo only comes over time, as a child matures, and as you teach them.

Wees

1. A newborn baby is totally unaware of when it needs to do a wee, and of when it is doing or has done one.

2. Babies' bladders need emptying up to 20 times a day, but they don't know the wee's coming, and they can't wait.

3. As the months pass, some babies dislike being in a wet nappy, but have no idea why their nappy is suddenly soggy.

Poos

1. As all parents and carers know, babies fill their nappies whenever they need to without knowing or caring that you've just changed it.

2. For at least a year, babies will fill their nappies several times a day, but have absolutely no awareness of having done so.

3. Gradually, a child usually begins to show you that they are about to do a poo, perhaps by grunting, straining, or a red face.

Ages and stages

It's probably fair to say that most people don't spend much time thinking about how they know whether they need to go to the toilet. (For the record, the relevant parts of our bodies send 'signals' to our brains that tell us.) For a child, however, learning to understand these bodily signals is as much of a learning curve as anything else they have to do.

When and where

The main stages a young baby goes through when learning to understand bodily signals are listed on the left of this page. Most babies realize when they have done a poo in their nappy before they know when they have done a wee in it, but this can vary a great deal. Some children remain completely oblivious of the contents of their nappy for much longer than others.

If you want to find out more, there's information about how our bodies work, and how specific muscles interact with our brains to prompt us to use the toilet at the Usborne Quicklinks Website (see page 61).

For many months babies do what they need to do in a nappy without even knowing about it.

In their own time

Some children so dislike a wet or dirty nappy that they do learn faster than others to use a potty, or toilet. Others will happily sit in a smelly nappy for hours, if you let them. Every child is different, and will learn what's expected of them in their own time, with your support. The process is gradual, but it does happen in several clearly-defined stages, over time. To help you know what to look for, there's a chart that shows roughly what to expect a child to be able to do, and when, on pages 55 to 57 of this book.

Experts have found that boys are often slower to respond to their bodies' messages about toileting than girls. This book has extra information, and tips for training little boys, wherever it is relevant and may help you.

Help me learn

Your main aim is to help small children begin to understand their bodies' signals, and this will take time, and patience. Of course, it can be irritating when a just-changed baby poos all over the changing mat or a little boy wees on you before you can get another nappy on him, but remember that, for them, going to the toilet is anything but private, or controllable. Bladder control and the idea of privacy are just two more of the many things they have to learn.

Some older babies are fascinated with what goes on in their nappies.

Useful tip
It helps babies to become aware of what their bodies are producing if you tell them what you find in their nappies (see also page 16).

It's your choice

Once you start thinking about potty-training your child, you may start searching out books and websites with expert advice on the best way of doing it. It can be a minefield of different opinions and tactics, all of which make it harder for you to know what to do. These pages look at the four main approaches to potty-training.

Starting early

In the days before washing machines and disposables, people tended to potty-train early – sometimes when babies were only a few months old. The idea of dangling a tiny baby over a potty may seem odd, but this method is used exclusively in some parts of the world, and there are people who favour starting well before the 18 to 24 months most experts suggest as the very earliest age to try.

A baby below this age won't really understand what's happening, won't be able to dress and undress themselves, and will have little control over when they wee or poo, so this method has big disadvantages.

Early training does mean fewer nappies to buy and throw away, or wash. (A baby can get through at least 5,000 before being toilet-trained.)

Tell me when you're ready

Some people argue that you should wait for your child to let you know when they are ready to come out of nappies. This method has the advantage of giving you some stress-free months when others around you may be knee-deep in soggy pants, and perhaps keeping some children happier in some ways, but there are downsides.

Most children naturally arrive at the point where they are ready to be potty-trained. The signs to look for are listed on pages 20 to 21. Others need a little more coaxing, and handing control of when to begin the training process over to a child can feel quite risky. There is much to recommend this method, but it can cause problems, too.

Bathroom

Sometimes, a child will let you know when they are ready to start being potty-trained.

Intensive training

Parents and carers are always busy, so the idea of intensive potty-training, or choosing a day to take nappies off and staying indoors until a child successfully uses the potty, is very appealing. A child still needs to be physically and emotionally ready to embark on this process, so it's best to avoid such quick fixes unless you are fairly sure that this is the case. Training a child intensively may limit the days of accidents and mopping up, but as children are all different, there's unlikely to be a miraculous intensive programme that will work successfully for every child.

See how it goes

This is the approach most parents and carers adopt, and the one this book suggests. It fits in most easily with normal life, and allows you to go out when you need to. It involves gradually preparing a child to come out of nappies, trying them on a potty, mopping up lots of accidents and, probably, still using nappies when you go out. Its advantages are that neither the adult nor the child is under enormous pressure, but it can take time for a child to get the message.

Useful tip
You'll find more detail about different approaches to potty-training, and what steps you need to follow for each one, on pages 58 to 59.

Whichever way you choose to handle training, it's something you and your child do together.

Comparing your child's progress to other children's is natural, but remember that no two children are exactly the same and it's not a competition.

Children need to be willing and ready to use the potty. You can't force them to do so.

You're the boss

Unfortunately, it can be very easy to get uptight about potty-training. You may find that you really mind if a friend's child is out of nappies before yours, or a relative makes you feel you're a failure if there's still a pack of disposables in your home. This page has some tactics to help you resist the pressures of potty-training.

Hurry up

If they are honest, most parents and carers worry that their child will lag behind others in their development. They wait eagerly for that first word, or first step, and are relieved when they come. They are even happier if their child's progress is roughly the same as other children of a similar age. Toilet-training is as much a part of a child's developmental progress as anything else, but problems getting a child out of nappies can make parents and carers feel inadequate. They may start to wonder if they should try to force a child to perform on a potty, though they would never dream of forcing a child to crawl, or walk, before they seemed ready.

Children come first

The unavoidable fact is that a child has to be ready to start potty-training. Most also need lots of encouragement, and, simply, to be trained. If they are not ready, you'll probably confuse, annoy and bore them. You may actually delay toilet-training success and could even traumatize them, by pushing it on them too soon.

It can be hard to hold your nerve if you are surrounded by parents of nappy-free toddlers, or people who feel they have a right to tell you how to do things. You may feel a stab of failure when someone makes a comment about your child still wearing a nappy, for instance. Remember that your child's needs, and happiness, are more important than what anyone else thinks, or any other child does.

12

Getting ready

Now that you know a little more about some of the possible pitfalls of potty-training, and how to survive them, this part of the book has some practical suggestions to help you both get ready to begin. They aim to ensure a smooth transition from nappy to potty, and should help a child understand a lot more about what's going to happen.

Help and advice

How and when to introduce a child to potties

What sort of potty to buy and how many

Useful tips for keeping a child relaxed
about their toileting needs

Advice on what words to use to talk
about toileting

Signs that show when a child is ready
to be potty-trained

The potty needs to become just another part of everyday life for your child.

Potty pals

The main piece of equipment you need to potty-train your child is, of course, a potty. In fact, it's a good idea to get one before you even begin training, so that it's familiar, and not new or scary, when it's time for your child to use it as you want them to. Here are some suggestions to help make your child more comfortable with the whole idea of using a potty.

Which potty?

Unfortunately, buying a potty is not as simple as it sounds. There's now such a huge range available, that it can be hard to know which one to choose. Manufacturers make potties that play a tune, light up, look like chairs, or are shaped like dogs or frogs, but none of them guarantees any more success than the most basic design. (In fact, it's probably not a good idea to encourage your child to go to the toilet on something that looks like a chair, anyway.) As a general rule, a potty is a means to an end, and, hopefully, won't be used for very long. Avoid spending a lot of money on one unless you are really convinced it will entice your child to use it more readily. On the left are four potty design essentials to bear in mind.

Potty design

• Make sure that the potty is light, but sturdy.

• A hole, or handle, makes carrying easier.

• If it's a bright colour, it may be more appealing.

• A raised lip will help stop wee splashing out.

Talk to your child about how the arrival of a potty in the house means that they are becoming a big boy or girl.

Introducing the potty

Some experts argue that the more potties you have around your home, the more likely your child is, eventually, to use one. It seems sensible to make sure you put a potty in the bathroom, near the toilet. If you want to put a potty in other rooms, it may mean less sprinting to fetch one later on, but will also mean that no part of your home will be a potty-free zone for a while.

When you introduce the potty, tell your child what it is, and that they will, one day, do their wees and poos in it. If they seem keen, let them sit on it whenever they want to, either in or out of a nappy. Your aim is to make them comfortable with their potty and the idea of sitting on it, so allow them some freedom to get to know it. For them, the whole business can be quite exciting, which is something for you to encourage.

Children often enjoy the novelty of sitting on their potty, though they may not use it for a while.

Potty care

It is important to keep potties clean, even before they are used properly. Don't let children put a potty near their mouth, or put food in it. The message to get across from the very beginning is that potties are where big boys and girls do wees and poos. The potties may become familiar objects after a while, which is good, but they do have a particular function. Make sure your child is always aware that potties are not for playing with, and aim to keep high standards of potty hygiene.

Potty-training will be a lot easier if you accept that potties, and toilets, will play a central role in both your lives.

Toilet talk

Not everybody feels at ease talking about what goes on in the toilet, but as the parent or carer of a small child, you may well find that you have to be. Talking about wees, poos, nappies, potties and toilets openly from their baby days onwards helps a child prepare for potty-training. Remembering this might help you abandon grown-up sensibilities for a while and just be prepared to talk about toilets a great deal.

What's in your nappy?

It may sound odd, but it's a good idea to make babies aware of what they've done in their nappies. There's no need to make an announcement, but talking about, and even showing them, what they have produced can help prevent a child being shocked when they see it later on, in the bottom of a potty.

Most people use phrases such as 'You've done a poo' completely naturally as they change a child's nappy. However, saying anything negative, or showing real distaste for what you find in a nappy, can make babies feel ashamed, confused or scared. This could make potty-training much harder for both of you, later on.

As you change your child's nappy, chat about what's in it in a positive, reassuring tone.

Everybody does it

Try to get everyone important in a child's life involved in talking as naturally as possible about going to the toilet. Keep it part of everyday life, rather than putting too much emphasis on it. There are some tips to help you on the right.

Two's company

Children copy what they see happening around them. Just as they mimic household tasks, such as sweeping and emptying shopping bags, so they watch and learn from what you do in the toilet – whether you want them as your audience or not. Once a baby can crawl, most parents have to get used to having company every time they go to the toilet. If you long for privacy at such times, take comfort from the fact that it's helpful for your child to be involved in your trips to the toilets and that they learn from them. Forget modesty: tell your child when you need to use the toilet, let them come too, and show them how things are done when you get there.

Some experts go further, suggesting that you give a running commentary on what you do in the toilet; the best advice is probably to do what feels natural for you. Your aim is to get babies used to the fact that people go somewhere special to wee and poo and that the whole business is entirely normal.

For a crawling baby, nowhere you go is private. They want to be where you are.

Show me how

• Encourage older siblings to let toddlers go with them into the toilet. The urge to copy what older children do is a strong learning incentive.

• Little friends who are further along in their potty-training might enjoy showing your child what they do on their potty or in the toilet.

• Fathers and big brothers can help little boys a lot. Even a baby in nappies will learn from watching Dad doing a wee while standing up.

• Some dolls wee out water when fed with a bottle. These might seem gimmicky, but if they help a child get the message, that's fine.

Useful tip

Most small children need little encouragement to talk about wee and poo. Within limits, just let them.

'Pee', 'wee' or 'number one'?

Encouraging a child to be comfortable talking about what their body produces, either in a nappy or potty, is all very positive, but it's a good idea to set some limits in this area, too. This page gives you some ideas for setting a few ground rules, so that children begin to learn what is acceptable for them to say and do, and what is not.

Which words?

Small children have little idea which words are polite, and which are rude. If you are thinking about potty-training a child, you need to decide what you are going to call the key things you'll need to talk about. Your child will copy the words you choose, so choose with care. Remember that you'll need words for urine, faeces, the vagina, the anus, the penis and for breaking wind. You'll need words that you're happy to use in public, as your child is unlikely to wait for a quiet moment to say them to you discreetly. Lastly, you must be prepared to hear these words often, as they may fascinate a child for quite some time.

Some people prefer to use more child-friendly words, such as 'wee-wee' and 'poo-poo'. Others prefer 'number 1' or 'number 2', and some choose the, reasonably bland, 'wee' and 'poo', which this book uses. There are families who choose to use the proper names, such as vagina and penis, for body parts. As long as everyone in your child's life uses the same words, without embarrassment, there should be no problems.

Useful tip

The toilet words you choose are up to you, but try picturing you and your child in a busy supermarket when you make that choice.

Children should not be made to feel self-conscious about wees and poos.

Ssshhh...!

However you describe going to the toilet, it's worth emphasizing that young children do not yet share your ideas of politeness, or discretion. If they need to go to the toilet, or have just been, they will tell you – probably loudly.

It's as well to accept right at the start that good manners are something we all learn over time. Try not to be cross with a child who announces to everybody on the bus that he has just done a poo. Remember that everyone was a small child once, so few people are likely to be offended.

For a child, their needs are always urgent. They haven't yet learned to wait for a good time to tell you about them.

Potties are everywhere

Talking about potties, wees and poos is always interesting for a child, but probably less so for you. Luckily, there are lots of good children's books and DVDs to help you vary the way you tackle the subject. They can make it more friendly and familiar, as they often have simple stories about children using potties in the 'wrong' way and doing silly things with them.

Useful tip

It's important to keep your child motivated, and keen to succeed in using their potty properly.

These funny potty stories are a great way of making clear to young children what is appropriate (sitting on the potty), and what is not (putting the potty on your head). Phrases such as 'You don't do that with *your* potty, do you?' help them understand what they should, and shouldn't, do with a potty. It gives them a sense of being big, and responsible, too. You'll find some suggestions for potty-based stories and other resources on the Usborne Quicklinks website (see page 61).

Books about potties show children that they are not the only ones using them.

19

Are you ready?

It can be difficult to pinpoint the ideal time to do more than just let a child become familiar with potties, and to start potty-training for real. Every child is different, but there are some signs you can look for to help you make an intelligent guess as to when to begin. Picking a time that suits you both is important (though it can be easier said than done). The following pages look at times when you may be ready to start and also at times when it's probably better to avoid trying to potty-train your child.

There can be no fail-safe checklist to tick off that will ensure that your child is ready to come out of nappies, but you may notice, over a period of several months, some of the signs which are listed on the left.

Ready to try?

• Is your child able to follow simple instructions you give them, such as 'go and fetch your shoes, please' ?

• Are your child's nappies dry for longer periods of time? This can mean that they are gaining more bladder control.

• Do they tell you that they've done a wee or poo? Some babies don't like being in dirty nappies, and pull them off.

• Is your child starting to let you know when they need to wee or poo? If so, training them should be even easier.

• Are they interested in what goes on in the toilet, and keen to try sitting on the potty or toilet themselves?

You can often tell when a child is filling their nappy from the expression on their face, or noises they may make (as well as the smell!).

Even though there are signs that a child may be physically and emotionally ready to start potty-training, very few children display all of them at the same time. Boys, in particular, tend to mature later in several ways, and may be slower to reach each stage.

Trial run

If your child is doing some of the things listed on the previous page, it might be a good idea to let them have a short time each day, say an hour or so, without a nappy on. Choose a similar time, perhaps after a meal, show them their potty, and tell them that's where they need to wee and poo. Don't be surprised, or cross, if they forget to use it at all, however. This tells you that it's best to wait a little longer before starting training.

During these months, when children seem almost ready to try without nappies, many people decide to put them in disposable trainer nappy pants. These are elasticated nappies that can be taken up and down like pants. It's not a good idea to use them at this stage, as most children treat them as they do a nappy, and freely wee and poo in them. See page 32 for when you might choose to use trainer pants.

Avoid cold weather

It's unrealistic to expect that all children will come out of nappies during fine, warm weather. However, it is sensible to avoid a period of freezing wintry weather for your child to spend more and more time out of nappies (and probably their trousers). Small children get cold very quickly.

Most toddlers are more than happy to spend some time without their clothes on, whether they are in nappies or not.

Think twice

For most children, potty-training involves a big change in their lives. You are asking them to learn to do quite a few new things, all at the same time. Sometimes, however keen you are to get rid of nappies, it can be more sensible to wait before starting potty-training. The main reasons for holding off a while are listed on the left. This page helps you decide if waiting might be best for you and your child.

Why wait?

Looking after small children is hard work, and potty-training adds to that. For a child to be successful in learning how to use the potty, the whole experience should be as positive as possible. If you feel that there are reasons why you might not be able to ensure that this is the case, wait a while. It will be best for both of you.

Small things can affect the training process a great deal. Starting on a Friday might mean you have more help over the weekend, for instance. Your mood, and energy levels, can have a big impact on things as well.

If a new baby has recently arrived, it may be easier to wait to train your toddler.

Reasons to wait

• Wait if you are especially tired, stressed, or have a very busy period ahead at work.

• If you are pregnant, or have just had a baby, you might feel stronger in a few weeks.

• Wait if you are planning a holiday, or to visit a potty-less, cream-carpeted house soon.

• If your child's behaviour is tricky at present, wait until they are in a calmer phase.

• Wait if your child seems unwilling to try training, or to be without their nappy on.

Training can wait

If, for any reason, you really feel that mopping up after your child might just be the last straw right now, it's better to postpone potty-training. Unlike a newborn baby needing a night feed, potty-training can wait for a few weeks without anybody coming to any harm.

Taking the plunge

By now, you've bought the potty, encouraged your child to sit on it, talked endlessly about wees and poos, and let them enjoy some nappy-free time. The next part of the book looks at the day you decide to say goodbye to nappies during the day and start training for real. This stage will be easy for some people; others find it more difficult.

Before you begin

Guidance on what to do on the first day
your child is without nappies

Lots of tips on how to keep going when things
get tough, or you get fed-up

Advice on how to encourage a child who
is finding training hard

Tips on how to handle going out
with a nearly-trained child

Most small children will be excited at the prospect of wearing their very own pants.

The big day

Everything that you and your child have done so far to get them used to the idea of using the potty is in preparation for the day that you decide to take your child out of nappies for good. This is a big step for them, and perhaps for you, too. These pages guide you through that very first nappyless day.

Choosing pants

Of course, before you actually take off your child's nappies, you need to make sure you've bought them some pants to wear instead. Most children will enjoy choosing their own, and doing so can make them reluctant to get them wet or dirty. It certainly makes a happy final step in their pre-potty-training preparations.

Day one

It's up to you to help make this first nappyless day as positive as possible. Here are four tips to help you.

1. Before you begin, make sure you have plenty of old, comfy clothes ready for your child to wear.

2. Tell your child that they are going to wear big boy's/girl's pants from today, and how proud you are of them.

3. Put their potty, or potties, where you want them to be. Show them to your child and tell them what's expected.

4. To minimize stress, have a mop, bucket, disinfectant and cloths to hand for quick clean-ups.

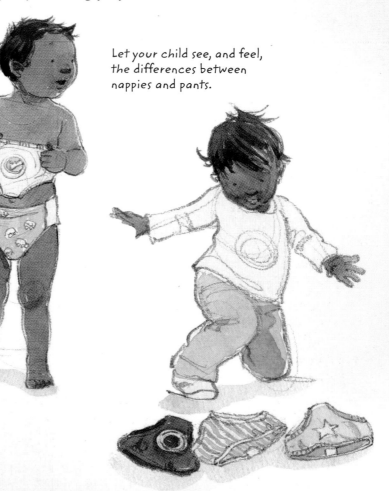

Let your child see, and feel, the differences between nappies and pants.

Watch and wait

The next step, after dressing your child in their new pants and suitable clothing, is to watch and wait. It's a good idea to prompt them to sit on the potty reasonably frequently, but don't interrupt their play to ask if they need to do so too often. This may just make them resentful and bored.

Remember that you're aiming for your child to understand and respond to their body's signals themselves, so avoid intervening too much at this early stage. You will, of course, have their toileting needs very much in mind during the day, but try not to let this take over. Make sure you both have some happy, potty-free time too.

Children often learn from what they see others doing.

Accidents do happen

There are bound to be accidents. A few children come out of nappies and start weeing and pooing in a potty straight away, but the vast majority need time to learn to interpret, and control, what their body needs to do.

You may be lucky, and catch most of the wees and poos a child does in the potty, but if not, don't make them sit on a potty until they do something. They will just get cold, fed-up and be less willing to sit on it again. You can encourage reluctant potty-sitters to stay on it for a little longer by reading them a favourite book, but a few minutes is probably the longest they should sit there.

Aim to handle any accidents the day brings calmly. Mop up with hot, soapy water, and put any wet clothes straight into the washing machine (rinsing dirty ones off first), to wait for your next load. If it's a warm day, you could let a child play in just their pants to reduce extra washing.

Useful tip
For daytime naps, put your child in nappies or put some padding, such as towels, under them.

Mopping up puddles is not much fun, but this stage of training won't last forever.

Keeping going

Your child may have got through one whole day without a nappy, but it can be hard to face more puddle-mopping and pant-washing on the days that follow. It's best to accept at the outset that, for most children, the training process is gradual, and takes time. Here are some ideas to help iron out some common early setbacks, and help you keep going.

Useful tip
If you need to leave the house during these early stages, see pages 32 and 33 for tips.

Gentle reminders

Remember that your attitude to training makes a big difference. Praise your child every time they manage to tell you that they need the potty, and do something in it. Don't go too over the top, however – just let them know that you are pleased with them.

One of the main mistakes people make if a child is regularly not getting to the potty in time is to remind them to sit on it more often. This is natural, but can be counter-productive. Some children stop trying to make it to the potty themselves, and others say they need it just to see you jump up to fetch it.

Keeping your cool

It's important to try to be consistent in your approach (which can be hard as you become steadily more frazzled). Aim to establish some very basic potty-routines in your household, and try to stick to them.

It's a good idea to bear in mind that, in most cases, children want to please the people who care for them. Many become so worried about their parents getting cross if they don't make it to the potty in time that they'll ask them for it without really needing it – which will make you cross anyway! It's important to see things from your child's point of view as much as you can.

It's fine to ask children to help you mop up, but don't make it seem like a punishment.

Say how you feel

It's easy to feel tired and frustrated if your child is creating extra work for you. It's also acceptable to tell them so, as long as you use phrases that won't scare them, such as 'I'm tired, Sam. Next time, try doing it in the potty.'

If you do lose your temper at the umpteenth puddle on the floor that morning, don't feel guilty. Nobody has endless patience, however good their intentions.
Say sorry with a hug, start again and remember that few children have accidents deliberately.

There's bound to be more washing during potty-training, but it won't always be like this.

Potty-training is a learning curve for both of you, so don't expect too much of yourselves.

Step back

Children can quickly switch off if they are confused about what they are supposed to do. Sometimes, a child starts off well, but then gets involved in other, more exciting, things, and forgets all about sitting on the potty. If this is happening to you and your child, or you are getting very stressed about their continuing accidents, step back and try the tactics on the right to help you keep calm.

Keep calm

• Count slowly to ten before saying anything when you find the latest puddle or poo.

• Have a phrase you always say, such as 'Never mind. It was an accident', for example.

• Take a really long, deep breath before walking away to get the mopping-up kit.

• If you are really worn out, can someone else do potty duty for a while?

Survival tactics

If all goes well for a few days, and the successes outnumber the accidents, you'll probably be feeling pretty good about deciding to try potty-training your child. If this is the case, you are lucky. For many people, things don't go this smoothly. On these pages, you'll find some tactics to try if you've hit a tricky phase, and are feeling thoroughly fed-up with potty-training.

Don't despair

• Think about whether your child is actually having that many accidents. Keep a note of exactly what goes on in a day. You may find things are not as bad as you had thought, and feel a bit better.

• If you are surrounded by potty-trained toddlers, it's easy to feel that you and your child have failed. Stay positive, and keep reminding yourself that different children have different needs.

• Talk to other people, who have been through this. Did they have similarly shaky times? Feeling that you're not the only one may be all you need to encourage you to keep mopping and washing.

Rewards

If things are not going well, and the days are passing without much progress, the ideas on the left might help you see things in a more positive light. To encourage your child, think about whether offering a small 'prize' for each successful trip to the potty might help motivate them.

Avoid making a trip to sit on the potty a punishment. You need your child to stay willing.

You could draw up a 'star chart', and explain to your child that every wee or poo in the potty will earn them a star, with perhaps every six stars earning them a small reward. What that reward may be is often less important to the child than the fact that they could win it. Simple treats, such as letting them pour lots of bubbles into their bath, often work well.

Remember not to get cross if your child still can't manage to make it to the potty. They will have wanted to get those stars, and that reward, just as much as you wanted them to. Make light of it, and keep encouraging them.

If you use a star chart, explain how the stars add up.

Problem-solving

It can be hard to analyse exactly what's going wrong when you're in the middle of it all. Below are three common problems that are easily solved.

Keeping a potty close at hand often jogs a child's memory to use it.

• If a boy regularly misses the potty, check the lip is at the front of the potty. Is his penis pointing downwards, so that wee flows into the potty?

• If a child regularly has accidents in a particular place or room, can you put a potty there? You can move it later but it might help now.

• If a child regularly wees or poos after a meal, make sure they always go on the potty then. Each success they have will encourage you both.

Trust yourself

Problem-solving tactics are all very well, but you do need to trust yourself. However determined you are to crack potty-training, you can't force a child to use the potty. You may need to re-think after a while if things are becoming very stressful and accidents are still outnumbering successes by a long way. It's better to have another go in a few weeks, or months, than make your child miserable. Perhaps they were not quite ready after all, and children learn things in their own good time, and not necessarily when you want them to. Pushing them when they're unwilling or unable to do something is utterly pointless and will make you both unhappy.

Useful tip
It can help to keep remembering that just about everyone gets there in the end and very few children start school in nappies.

Keeping a trusting, happy relationship with your child is more important than anything else.

Getting there

If a child is ready to be potty-trained, they usually master it quite quickly – often within the first few days. Gradually, the number of accidents lessens, and the number of wees and poos in the potty increases. These pages look at the next stage of training, as the potty becomes part of daily life.

Over to them

If you feel that your child is coping well, you can start to remind them to sit on the potty less often. As they develop more control over their bladder and bowels, they should start to find the potty themselves when they need it. If your child tends to need to wee as soon as they have told you they do, keep reminding them about the potty fairly regularly, however, as not getting there in time might discourage them.

You will have to supervise wiping a child's bottom for quite a while, especially if they are at the younger end of the potty-training age range (i.e. under two years old). You'll also almost certainly have to supervise hand-washing too, and may still have to help out with pants, tights or trousers. There's more about teaching children these extra toileting skills on pages 38 and 39 of this book.

Keep dressing your child in clothes that are easy for them to pull down...

... and up again.

Over time, most children gain more and more independence in using the potty.

Useful tip
Don't remind your child to use the potty more than once every 15 minutes.

Spread the news

Most children are extremely proud of themselves every time they do something in the potty. If you praise them, and let them help you empty the potty and flush the contents away, they will be even more so. A few children don't tell people when they have done a wee or poo, so their potties will need regular checking. Usually, however, children announce their toileting achievements with gusto.

It's a good idea to let your child tell other people in their lives that they now do wees and poos in the potty. It can really increase their self-esteem and help them see how positive their behaviour is. They could telephone a grandparent or a friend to tell them how well they are doing, for instance.

Amongst the successes, there are bound to be accidents. Many children still have them months after they last wore a nappy. Don't make a big deal about such slips, or draw attention to what's happened in front of others. Deal with the situation calmly, and show your child that you know that their accident was just that – an accident.

If your child tells you all about what they have done in the potty, listen, and congratulate them. For them, it's very important.

False start

Some children have a faultless first few days of potty-training, then have a period of time with lots of accidents. This can be a sign either that they are not quite mature enough to understand what they need to do, or that they can't yet remember to do it in time, every time. Whatever the reason, it's very frustrating.

If your child follows this pattern, and things don't improve again soon, you may need to go backwards a little in the training process. Give them some time in, and out, of nappies, and see how things go for a while before trying training again. They will get there, in their own time.

Stand or sit?

Little boys are often keen to wee like Daddy does, standing up. Unless your child is really reluctant to use a potty, it's probably best to wait until they have some degree of control over where they wee before letting them do it standing up.

Going out

Even if you opt to stay at home for the first few days your child is out of nappies, you will eventually need to venture out. These pages help you make sure that going out with a partly-trained child is as easy as it can be.

Two choices

For most parents, not going out at all for several days is simply not an option. They may have to make local trips, such as to fetch another child from school or nursery, for example. If these circumstances apply to you, you have two main choices about how to handle these unavoidable, short outings with your nearly-trained child: you can either put them in a nappy or trainer pants, or take a risk, and take them out in just their clothes. To help you choose, the pros and cons of both options are shown on the left.

Many toddlers cope better than you might expect without a nappy on.

Nappy or not?

• If you decide to put your child back into a nappy or trainer pants, you may confuse them. This is convenient, but not very consistent, so don't choose this option on a regular basis.

• If you decide to take a risk, tell your child that you're going out and sit them on the potty. Tell them to try to do a wee now, but don't make them stay there too long.

Useful tip

Just before you go anywhere, encourage your child to sit on the potty and try to 'go'.

Be prepared

If you want to go further afield, for longer, with a nearly-trained child, you need to be prepared. It's best not to put your child in trainer pants to go out for long: most children use them just like nappies, which is a backwards step in their training. The same applies to the, once popular, plastic-lined trainer pants (which are not very absorbent, either).

Think about where you're going: this may not be the time to visit a childless friend with an immaculate house. Wherever you're going together, remember that the worst thing that could happen is that your child soaks, or dirties, their clothes, their buggy and/or car seat, and perhaps even your lap. On the right are some ways of dealing with these things, if they happen.

Little and often

Dealing with a damp, distressed small child in public is not easy. Don't worry about whipping out the potty when your child needs it: that's far better than a wet floor. For a while, you may have to accept less ambitious trips out, and expect frequent potty-stops along the way.

If outings prove really difficult, remember that this phase will not last forever. Once children are happy to use a toilet, things get easier, as the next section of this book will show you. Before then, be reassured that your child will learn to control their toileting needs, but that the only way for them to do so is to keep practising. It's important for both of you to get out and about regularly while you are potty-training.

Preparation checklist

• *Take at least one change of dry clothing for your child with you (including socks).*

• *Take several plastic bags, wipes, and a potty hooked over buggy handles.*

• *Cover buggies or car seats with towels, unfolded nappies or taped-down plastic bags.*

• *If getting a damp lap would cause real problems, take dry clothes for yourself too.*

You'll still need to take a changing bag whenever you go out for a while, but it will contain dry clothes, not nappies.

33

'I need a wee!'

These words can strike panic into most parents, but even more so if your child is in the middle of potty-training. If you've simply forgotten to bring a potty, and your child needs to go, you'll need to think fast, as they probably can't wait long. On the left are three tips for coping with such toileting emergencies, and there's more guidance below.

However inconvenient it may be, it's important not to let a small child become anxious about the timing of their bodily functions. Trying to hold on, or worrying about having an accident, can lead to serious, longer-term problems.

If a child says they need to go, they usually mean it. Explain that there isn't a potty for them to use, but that you are going to help them use the toilet. You may have to hold them over it, but it's good to get them used to this early on. Not all public toilets are as clean as you might wish, but, with small children, you may not have a choice.

If there's a queue for the toilet, explain your child's situation. Most people will let them go first.

It's private

Going to the toilet is a private thing, and it's important to teach children this. If a child is desperate to wee, however, and the only option (other than wet pants) is to hold them over a drain or at the roadside while they do so, it's best simply to explain what has to happen, and help them – as discreetly as you can. This is not ideal, but it's just part of life with a small child. It's far better than causing them any anxiety or discomfort.

Useful tip
It's a good idea to have some anti-bacterial wipes or evaporating hand-cleaning gel with you at all times.

Time for the toilet

There is no right time for a child to start using the toilet. Most use a potty before they do so, others miss out potties and go straight to the toilet. A few use both potties and toilets. This part of the book looks at how to introduce a child to using a toilet, whenever you decide to do it.

A step up

Advice on how to make sure a child is happy about starting to use the toilet

Information about equipment that will make it easier for your child to use the toilet independently

How to establish a 'toilet routine', including hand-washing and bottom-wiping

Tips and techniques to help little boys use the toilet successfully

For a small child, there's a lot to remember to do each time they go to the toilet.

Using the toilet

For some children, making the transition from the potty to the toilet is easy; for others it takes longer. These pages offer some guidelines to help get your child on the path towards being able to use the toilet independently.

Children often feel happier sitting on a child-sized toilet trainer seat.

Disadvantages

• There may not be a toilet nearby exactly when your child needs one. They may have to learn to wait.

• Many public toilets are dirty, and not at all child-friendly. Find out the best ones in your area.

• Your own toilet will need to be extra clean for a while as your child will be touching it often.

• Some children are scared of the flush, or of falling into the toilet. There are tips to help on page 37.

Pros and cons

If your child seems ready and willing, give them the chance to try using a toilet. Some small children prefer to sit on the toilet rather than a potty from the very beginning, but you'll need to make sure it's accessible for them, and hold them securely on the toilet seat. Just as when children start using potties, there may be accidents during the early days. A child may not sit back far enough on the toilet seat, or may just not get their pants down in time.

There are many advantages to children using the toilet, but there are some disadvantages too (listed on the left). Overall, once your child can use a toilet, things are much easier. You don't need to carry a potty everywhere, or have them dotted around your house. You won't need to empty full potties any more, either, and flushing the toilet is much less of a chore. Remember that when your child can manage their own toileting needs, your job will be done.

Watch and learn

Your child will probably have seen you use the toilet countless times, but it's still a good idea to take the time to make sure they are comfortable about sitting on a toilet themselves before expecting them to do so regularly. You could start by putting their potty next to the toilet, and encouraging them to use it from time to time when you are using the toilet. It may sound odd, but it may really help your child feel relaxed. Let them pull the flush for you, or pass you some toilet paper when you need it. It's all valuable learning for them. If they seem willing, let them sit on the toilet occasionally (with nappies on at first if it makes them feel more secure). Tell them how everything is washed away by all the water when you flush the toilet.

Small children tend to use too much toilet paper, so keep a close eye.

Toilet problems

Sometimes children are frightened of sitting on the toilet, or the noise or splashing of the flush. There are some ways to tackle these fears listed on the right, but if nothing helps, it may be wiser to leave toilet-training for now. This phase is nothing to worry about and usually passes quickly.

Some children like watching the toilet flush and you need to be extra vigilant about toilet hygiene if they hold onto the bowl or seat.

Toilet fears

• Don't flush until your child is off the toilet seat. If they are nervous of the flush, wait until they are out of the room.

• Put sheets of toilet paper inside the toilet bowl to reduce upward splashes.

• Hold your child while they are sitting on the toilet, so that they feel secure.

Steps and seats

• Plastic steps like this one can help small children reach the toilet and basin.

• Trainer seats make sitting on a toilet much easier.

More toilet tips

Once your child has got used to sitting on the toilet, the ideas on these pages should help them learn to use it independently. Remember to keep things as low-key as possible, to help them feel happy and confident about being in charge of their own toileting needs. That's the main aim of all this training, after all.

Most toilets are designed for adults. They are too high for small children to get on and off easily on their own. The seats are bigger than their bottoms, too, which can make them feel that they might fall into the toilet bowl. Two inexpensive pieces of equipment solve both these problems. A plastic step helps children reach the toilet, and a plastic toilet trainer seat (which slots on top of the full-sized seat) fits a child's bottom and makes them feel safer.

Start to finish

Once a child can wee and poo in a toilet, they need to be able to do three more things: wipe their bottoms, flush the toilet and wash their hands. This will all take practice, and you will probably have to help them for some time to come, but aim to teach them this routine from the outset. These skills will be important for the rest of their lives.

Show your child how much toilet paper to use, and how to make a pad to wipe their bottoms. Toilet wipes are useful, but you need to teach children how to use paper, too, for when wipes are not available. It's more hygienic for both girls and boys to wipe their bottoms from the front to the back. Boys should gently shake their penis over the toilet.

Washing hands after using the toilet is essential basic hygiene, and cuts the risk of catching threadworms (see opposite page). It's important to teach your child that they need to wash their hands every time they have used the toilet.

Children copy what they see, and want to do things just like everyone else does.

About threadworms

Threadworms are tiny white worms that live mainly in and around the anus. They are very common, and symptoms include an itchy bottom and a lack of energy. You may see the worms in a child's poos. Threadworm eggs are laid around the anus, so hands that are not well washed after bottom-wiping can pick them up. If a child then sucks their unwashed fingers, or bites their nails, they may swallow the threadworm eggs, making the infestation worse. Threadworms are easy to kill with medicine or tablets from a pharmacist, and it's best for the whole family to be treated. A good hand-washing routine, plus keeping fingernails short, should keep them at bay.

Doggy licks

Dogs can pass on threadworms by licking a child's face or hands, so try to discourage this. Make sure children's hands are always washed after they have touched animals.

Make sure all children understand the importance of thorough hand-washing.

Boys' toilet tips

Little boys can benefit from some specific tips as they learn to use the toilet. If their dad, or an older brother, can show them what to do, so much the better. If aiming their penis into the toilet to wee is proving tricky, balls of screwed-up paper, or a bobbing cork in the toilet, give boys something to aim at. Teach boys how to lift the toilet seat and lid before they wee and make sure both are secure, in case they fall down and hurt them. Encourage boys not to drip wee on the floor, or leave lots of splashes on the rim. Aim to help them learn to use the toilet considerately from the start.

Using the toilet properly is a skill, like any other, that a child needs help to master.

For some children, getting out of, and back into, their clothes, is the trickiest part of a visit to the toilet.

Pride and praise

If your child visits the toilet and returns, dressed, with washed hands, you can congratulate yourself on having a child who is fully toilet-trained during the day. As always, where children are concerned, there may still be hiccups ahead, but focusing on positive things will encourage them, and help you deal with any setbacks.

Keep up the praise

Children thrive on praise, so, without over-doing things, remember to keep letting them know how proud you are of them using the toilet. Tell them that it's great for you not to have to change their nappies or empty potties any more and that you really appreciate what they are doing.

Many children enjoy the chance to show others that they are now too grown-up for a potty by handing it over to a smaller child. They will probably be extremely proud of the fact that they don't need it any more.

Relapses

Older children may start having more accidents when a new baby arrives. This phase usually passes quickly.

It's very common for children to have the odd accident, even after months out of nappies during the day. There can be a variety of reasons why this happens: they could be unwell, very absorbed in their play, or feeling nervous or unsure. One of the most common causes for relapses is a stressful event in a child's life, such as starting pre-school, the arrival of a new brother or sister, going into hospital or moving house.

If a child seems unwell, or is experiencing pain when they wee or poo, take them to a doctor straight away. If they seem well, but are just not getting to the toilet in time, try to be patient: offer reassurance, and wait for them to get back on track. If problems persist, you may have to consider going back to potties for a while, to re-establish some basic rules.

Problem solving

No childcare expert can guarantee that, even
if you follow a programme or list of instructions
to the letter, a child will be potty or toilet-trained
at the end of them. Many people encounter setbacks
along the way. This part of the book looks at
specific problems parents often face, and
offers help in solving them.

What's going wrong?

How to help children who are slower
becoming potty-trained than others

Guidance for when children are reluctant to do
a poo anywhere other than in a nappy

Tips for tricky situations, such as a child having
frequent accidents at nursery or when you are out

Advice on more serious problems, such as chronic
constipation or uncontrollable weeing

Common problems

On the next few pages, you'll find advice on solving the most common daytime potty-training problems. If you are very worried about your child's toileting behaviour, always ask a health professional for help.

Q: Why won't my child 'get' the potty-training message?

A: Parents often get extremely anxious if they feel that their child is taking longer to potty-train than others. This book emphasizes throughout how important it is that you stay positive, and don't put pressure on your child. Your getting stressed about it all will probably only delay toilet-training even further. Hard as it may be, some children just take longer than others. Follow the guidance in this book and be assured that your child will be clean and dry in the end.

Q: My child will not wipe her own bottom. When should I make her?

A: You'll do a much better job of this than most small children, so it's tempting to keep doing it, rather than letting them try. It is very important that a child's bottom is as clean as possible, to avoid soreness, germs and unpleasant smells. It's best to give them lots of practice in learning how to wipe their bottoms (before bathtime is a good time), but check how they have done until they are at least three years old. Once your child starts school, teachers won't have time to help them, so aim for them to be accomplished bottom-wipers by then.

Q: Why does my child keep pooing in his pants?

A: A few children soil their pants because they don't like using the potty or toilet, actively preferring to poo in their pants, but most do it because they are constipated. If they put off doing a poo (perhaps because of one painful experience), eventually, semi-liquid poo from behind the hard, more solid poo in their bowel leaks out into their pants. Make sure your child's diet includes lots of fruit and vegetables and plenty of fluids, as this helps prevent constipation. If the problem persists, see a doctor.

Q: Why does my child wet her pants at nursery, but not at home?

A: Many children have accidents when they're somewhere less familiar than home, and may need more frequent prompting to go to the toilet if they're busy playing. Talk to your child and to the staff (without your child overhearing) about what's happening. Perhaps your child is upset at nursery or dislikes the toilets? Keep sending dry clothes, don't get cross and keep praising potty successes at home.

Q: My 3 year-old was clean and dry, but now has lots of accidents, which is frustrating. What should I do?

A: Many children have relapses like this. The novelty of using the potty may have worn off. Talk to your child about what they should be doing, what they are doing and how uncomfortable wet clothes must be. Would they prefer only to use the toilet, or to move the potty somewhere else? If they want to go back into nappies, it may help to let them for a short time.

Q: Why will my child only poo in a nappy?

A: Some children go through a phase of not wanting to push a poo out into what feels like nothingness (i.e. the potty or toilet). We may find this difficult to understand, but it's vital to accept a child's worries and help them overcome them. Until this phase passes, lining the toilet with toilet paper can help, as can putting the child on the toilet only when they are more likely to need to poo, such as after a meal.

Children are quick to pick up on your anxiety if there are problems with toilet training, so stay calm and reassuring.

More problems

Q: I think my child is not using the potty deliberately. What can I do?

A: It's hard to know if a child is deliberately not getting to the toilet or potty in time. It may be that your child can see that their accidents get them attention from you, even if it is negative attention. Try not reacting to their accidents, but cleaning up without showing any emotion. If your child is old enough, getting them to help clean up (without getting cross) can work too. If they do use the potty, praise them and give them lots of positive attention whenever you can. This may help break the cycle.

Q: Now that he is wearing pants, my son has started playing with his penis a lot. Should I worry?

A: Small children are naturally fascinated with parts of their bodies, and it's entirely normal for boys and girls to touch their genitals, and discover that this can feel nice. The best approach is not to stop them, but to tell them not to touch these parts of their bodies in front of other people, as that's something that's best kept private. Forbidding it altogether might make it seem all the more appealing.

Q: I am getting extremely annoyed with my child every time she has an accident. What can I do?

A: Most children get distressed if their carer is cross with them. If potty-training is making your relationship suffer, is it worth persevering? Think about having a break from it, asking someone else to take over for a while or trying again another time when you feel more relaxed. There are also some tips to try on pages 26 and 27. You may both have got into a cycle of stress and upset which you need to break, as it's probably making you both very miserable.

Q: My child will only use our toilet at home. This makes going out very difficult. What should I do?

A: This problem may have sprung from just one negative experience when using another toilet (such as finding it dirty), but it is exasperating. You could hold your child above 'other' toilet seats, so that they make no contact with them at all. Using a toilet yourself first may also allay their fears, as can wiping it thoroughly for them. If all else fails, you may just have to keep taking a potty out with you, until they gain more confidence.

Q: I've tried potty-training my 3 ½ year-old several times but we still have wet pants. What shall I do?

A: It might be worth cancelling everything for a day or so and really focusing on training. As your child is old enough to go straight to the toilet, skip the potty and use the time to help them make the link between needing to use the toilet and getting to it in time. Praise any successes, and consider small prizes too. It could be a good opportunity to replace past negative attempts with an intensive, but positive, one.

Q: My 3 year-old girl isn't interested in coming out of nappies at all and gets very upset if I suggest using the potty. What can I do?

A: It's good that you're still 'suggesting' rather than 'forcing' her to use the potty, as this is one thing you can't make a child do. By the age of three, your child should be capable of being potty-trained, but may, for a variety of reasons, have pitted her will against yours and decided not to try. Follow the advice and guidelines in this book, and trust that, eventually, your child will join other children successfully out of nappies. If you've still made no progress by the time your daughter is four, ask a health professional.

Q: My 3 year-old son can't do a wee standing up. Will he ever do it?

A: Yes, if only when he sees other boys doing it at nursery, or at school, as he won't want to be different. If his dad, or an older brother can show your son how such things are done and let him have lots of practice himself, this will help. Otherwise, don't worry; he will learn in his own good time.

Asking for help

Sometimes a child may encounter problems such as those on this page, which need expert help to solve. If you are ever really worried about a child's toileting behaviour, remember that health professionals are there to help you, and have a lot of experience and expertise in all areas of child development, so ask for their help if you need it.

Chronic constipation

Many small children are constipated from time to time, or produce hard poos that hurt their bottoms. Time, a balanced diet, and plenty of fluids usually sort this out. In some cases, and for a variety of reasons, children get so distressed about pooing that they refuse to go at all for fairly long periods of time. Unfortunately, however, as their body's need to poo increases, so does their fear.

This cycle can lead to enormous distress for the child and those caring for them, but it can be solved with expert help. Doctors often prescribe mild laxatives to soften poo: these may have to be taken for some time, to help the child go to the toilet regularly and overcome their anxiety. Stay calm if your child is panicking about doing a poo, as your stress, plus their terror, will make their problem worse.

Wet pants

Some children are regularly unable to control the flow of urine from their bladder in time to reach a potty or toilet. They may soak their clothes and the floor without a moment's notice. This is embarrassing for them, especially if they're at school, and you need expert support to tackle it. There are several solutions, from writing 'Do I need a wee?' reminders on a child's palm, to medication that can control the flow of urine in children over six years old. Talk to your doctor or health visitor about which one will help your child. You'll find information about night-time bed-wetting, called enuresis, in the next part of the book.

It's very important to make sure your child's diet always contains plenty of fresh fruit and vegetables.

Infections

If a child is experiencing pain when they wee, is weeing much more often, or has cloudy wee, they may have an infection in their urinary tract. Girls are more prone to these. A course of antibiotics from your doctor will usually clear these infections up.

Dry nights

Most children are still wearing nappies
at night long after they are clean and
dry during the day. This part of the book
gives you some guidance in helping your
child learn how to be clean and dry
at night, as well.

Peaceful nights

How to know when your child is ready to come
out of nappies at night

Guidelines on getting your child, and their bed,
ready to try a nappyless night

Different tactics for overcoming any
setbacks you come across

Suggestions for dealing with the problem of
regular bedwetting in older children (known as enuresis)

Nights and nappies

As a general rule, most children are dry at night by their third birthday, but many continue to wear a nappy at night for much, much longer. It takes time to gain enough control to hold on, or to get up and go to the potty or toilet, during the night.

The night-time nappy can be hard to say goodbye to for some children, as it's very much a part of bedtime.

There's no rush to take off night-time nappies. Nobody except your family will know if your child wears one.

Most young children spend at least 12 hours in bed each night. That's a long time for them to last without doing a wee, so their bladder needs to be mature enough to cope. There's absolutely no point taking off night-time nappies unless you are fairly sure your child is ready to be without them. Some typical signs that they might be are on the left. Few children do all of these things, but if they do two of them, they may be ready to be nappyless at night.

Signs to spot

• Is your child waking up and telling you they need a wee?

• Is your child's night-time nappy dry most mornings?

• Is your child reluctant to put on a nappy at night?

• Does your child pull their nappy off during the night?

Soggy morning nappies

Many children who are almost ready to be dry at night wake up with a soaking nappy. The bladder is at its fullest in the morning, so it's common for a child to do a big wee just before, or just as, they wake up. If this is happening to your child, you could wake them up a little earlier for a few days and take them to the potty to wee there instead. If this stops them from weeing in their nappy, you can gradually make the wake-up time a little later each day.

Is 'lifting' a good idea?

Many people decide to try a technique called 'lifting' when they first stop putting their children in nappies at night. They feel it may lessen the risk of being woken in the small hours to change wet pyjamas and bedding. This process involves your gently lifting a sleeping child and taking them to sit on the toilet at some point during the night. Some people wake the child to walk to the toilet themselves, others carry them there. Most lift their child just before they go to bed themselves. Many people continue to practise lifting for several years, even when the child is less likely to have an accident during the night.

It is not easy to carry a child to the toilet without waking them up...

... or for a sleepy child to know what you want them to do.

Childcare experts are divided on whether lifting is a good idea or not, so the decision about whether to do it at all is up to you. It can save wet beds, and broken nights, for some families – certainly in the short term – but there are disadvantages. The main drawback is that the child is more asleep than awake throughout, so you are, in reality, encouraging them to wee in their sleep. Lifting a child will also disturb their sleep to some degree, and you may actually wake them right up. Weigh up the pros and cons carefully before you decide if lifting will work for you.

Children often sleep very deeply, and may not wake at all when you lift them at night.

49

The final nappy

The last nappy your child ever wears will probably be their night-time nappy. These pages guide you through putting your child to bed without a nappy for the first time. If you are prepared, and your child is keen to try being nappyless, they are much more likely to wake up in a dry bed. Don't expect miracles, though: there may well be a few accidents.

Bedtime preparations

On the left, you can read the steps you need to follow on the night you decide not to put a nappy on your child. Before you begin, explain that your child is a big boy or girl now, and doesn't need to wear a nappy any more. This won't guarantee success, but it's better to involve them from the start. Many people put a potty near their child's bed, in case they do need to go to the toilet in the night. Leaving a dim night-light on in their bedroom makes it easier for a child to find the potty. It also makes it less disruptive for you to go in and change wet bedding, should you need to.

At the ready

1. Put a waterproof mattress cover onto your child's cot or bed, under the sheet. They are easily sponged dry (unlike a wet mattress).

2. Have plenty of dry bedding and pyjamas to hand. Fumbling for them in the middle of the night will mean less sleep for both of you.

3. Don't worry about letting your child have a small drink near bedtime, but make sure they use the potty or toilet before they get into bed.

4. In the morning, take your child to the toilet or potty as soon as they wake up. If their bed is dry, give them plenty of praise. If not, try again.

It will take time for a child to recognize the signs of needing to wee or poo when they are fast asleep.

Not a good time

Few people are at their best when they are woken from a deep sleep to change wet sheets and pyjamas. Even fewer are gracious if this has happened several times. Many children will wake up, and wake you up, when they feel their bed is wet, whereas others will sleep on until morning, untroubled. Aim to keep things calm and dimly-lit as you do what needs doing. Changing wet beds in the middle of the night is not the best part of parenting, but it won't last forever.

Your child will probably be upset about having had an accident, will not like waking up in a cold, damp bed and will certainly not have wet themselves deliberately. If accidents persist, see page 52 for more information about regular bedwetting, or enuresis.

Try not to be too grumpy when your child wakes you up in the night.

Nights away

Children who have been nappyless at night for several months often have relapses when they are troubled about something, or when they are in an unfamiliar environment, such as someone else's house, and bed. If you're going to be away from home soon after a child has come out of night-time nappies, consider taking your own bedding including the waterproof mattress cover. You could also put extra padding, such as towels, under your child at night. If you are staying with other people, it's probably best to explain your child's situation when you arrive, as nobody will want you to worry.

Useful tip
Disposable nappy mats, that protect mattresses, are very useful for trips away from home.

Wet beds

Studies show that a surprising number of children wet their bed on a regular basis, so don't feel you are unusual, or alone, if your child is doing so. Regular bedwetting, or enuresis, can be distressing and disruptive for the whole family, but there are ways of dealing with it. This page offers you some help and advice.

When to worry

Experts usually don't consider bedwetting to be a problem until a child is over five years old, and most doctors will not suggest getting specialist help until after this age. There are various treatments available, (depending on why the child is wetting the bed) and most are successful.

If bedwetting is really troubling a young child, or affecting their self-confidence, consider asking for help earlier. Your health visitor may have some straightforward suggestions as to why your child is weeing while asleep. For instance, a small reward for each dry night can help, as some children simply don't feel like getting out of their warm bed at night to visit the toilet.

The last thing you want to do is to make any child anxious about wetting their bed as that can increase the likelihood of them doing it for longer. As long as it's sorted out before they need to sleep away from home on school trips, for example, don't let it become a major source of anxiety for anyone.

Boys and bedwetting

Research shows that little boys are more prone to bedwetting than girls, and that it seems to take them longer to gain enough bladder control not to need to wee during the night. Knowing this may help you stay patient as you change their wet bedding yet again.

Useful tip
If your child wets the bed regularly, have dry clothes and bedding ready, to make changing them as quick and calm as you can.

Boys mature more slowly than girls in several ways throughout childhood, and there's nothing you can do to change that fact.

Useful information

This, final, part of the book has information that you may find helpful as you potty-train a child. Some of the material here expands on subjects looked at on earlier pages, and some of it is new.

What will I find?

A step-by-step guide on how to potty-train, bringing together all the main points made in this book

Information about different approaches to training, and how to use them

General information about children with special needs, and suggestions as to how to use the internet as a support

A list of simple mistakes it's all too easy to make when potty-training a child (to help you not to make them)

One step at a time

This book emphasizes throughout that there is no single programme of potty-training that will guarantee success for every child. Each child is different and so are his or her family circumstances. However, it may be helpful to have the overall approach that this book suggests broken down into a series of easy-to-follow steps, so this is what you will find on the following pages.

You don't need to follow these steps rigidly: few children will allow you to, anyway. They are designed as a framework, a useful reference, as you train your child. You may find you miss out some steps completely, or do some in a different order. Every parent will work out their own ways of overcoming problems, and arriving at their goal: a happy, nappyless child. As you look through the steps, keep in mind that there may be several months between some stages, depending on how old, and mature, your child is.

Learning to use the potty is one of the many, many things your child has to learn.

Useful tip

Trust your instincts. Remember that you know your child better than anyone else does.

Things to remember

As you read the steps on the following pages, keep these three things in mind.

• Expect and accept setbacks and accidents. Potty-training is a learning process.

• Don't impose a training timetable that suits you, on your child. It's pointless.

• Make sure that your child understands what you want them to do, and be consistent.

Potty-training: start to finish

1

Experts don't recommend even trying to train a child until they are between 18 and 24 months old. Some children are mature enough to be trained by the age of two, but many are not.

2

Buy a potty (or several, if you wish) and talk to your child about what they are for. Explain that big girls and boys do poos and wees in them and that they will too.

3

Let your child become familiar with the potty and try sitting on it (in or out of a nappy). Don't let them play with it too much, though. It's not a toy.

4

When your child comes to the toilet with you, talk to them about what happens there. Choose, and use, the 'toilet words' you want them to say, with care. Children will repeat what they hear.

5

Encourage your child to tell you when they have done a wee or poo in their nappy. They usually learn this before they learn when they are going to do one.

6

If your child is willing, take their nappy off for a while. Get them to sit on the potty for a few minutes at a regular time each day, such as after a meal or before bed.

7

Look at children's books, and watch DVDs about potties, to help a child see what they are for and that they are a part of all kinds of children's lives.

Don't deny your child a drink if they need one.

8

Gradually increase the number of times your child sits on the potty. Make sure they drink plenty of fluids, so that they need to wee regularly.

9

Build up nappy-free time at home, making sure your child understands you would like them to do wees and poos in the potty now. Praise any successes they have, but don't expect too much of them.

10

Make a special shopping trip together to choose some new pants for your child. Remember to buy quite a few pairs so you don't have to do washing too often.

11

When your child seems ready, it's time to get rid of nappies. Explain what's going to happen and tell your child to tell you whenever they need the potty.

Children need to be reminded to sit on the potty if they are very involved in their play.

12

Remind them fairly frequently to use the potty, but don't interrupt their play too often. Your aim is for them to learn to know when they need to go for themselves.

13

Keep praising all successes in the potty, and aim to deal with accidents calmly. Remember that your child is learning lots of new skills at once.

14

When you go out, either put your child in a nappy, trainer pants, or put them on the potty just before you leave and go prepared to deal with any accidents. Most children will have a few.

15

You will need to wipe your child's bottom and supervise hand-washing for quite a while. Show them good hygiene habits until they can put them into practice for themselves later.

16

If all is going well, encourage your child to find the potty themselves when they need to go by reducing the frequency of your reminders. Consider offering a small reward for successful potty use.

17

If things are not going well, think about stopping training for a while. Don't risk making your child upset or fearful about the whole business. Many children need several attempts.

18

If your child is keen to use the toilet, a plastic child's toilet seat will fit their bottom better. A plastic step makes getting on and off the toilet easier for a small child.

19

Gradually, help children learn to wipe their bottom, flush the toilet, wash their hands and pull their pants, trousers or tights back up on their own. Check how they cope until you are confident they can manage.

20

If you are worried about any aspect of potty-training, or your child's behaviour and toileting needs, always ask your health visitor, or doctor, for advice.

When your child stops wearing a nappy at night, they are fully toilet-trained.

21

Aim to lose night-time nappies when your child's nappies are dry each morning, when they aren't keen to wear a nappy, or they get up to wee. Protect their mattress before you put them to bed nappyless.

Other approaches

This book suggests one approach to potty-training your child, but there are other methods. Here is more detail about the three other main methods parents use to train their babies and toddlers.

Baby training

In some parts of the world, especially in warm climates, babies don't wear nappies at all; they are held over a potty from birth. For this approach to work, parents need to learn to spot a baby's bodily signals, and predict when they need to go to the toilet in time to hold them over a potty. In developed countries, experts do not recommend this method of training, and it is unusual for parents to try it, but, for some people, it feels right. Here's how the method works.

It is vital to have a very good understanding of your child's needs and behaviour for the baby training method to work.

Signs and sounds

1. Parents study their baby's toileting habits closely, getting to know if they wee and poo at certain times, and interpreting signs that they need to go.

2. After some time, parents should, ideally, begin to know when it is the right time to hold their child over a potty by being 'in tune' with their child.

3. Some parents make a specific noise to encourage their baby to go to the toilet. Ideally, when the baby hears that sound, they will wee or poo.

4. Slightly older babies can learn to make certain signs or gestures that mean they need to use the potty. This takes time, and plenty of practice.

This method is better for the environment, as no nappies are used, but it requires an enormous commitment from parents. The time they invest may increase the emotional bond between them and their baby, but for a long while, the child will rely largely on the adult to know that they need to do a wee or poo, rather than understanding their needs themselves. Relapses are common, as are other toileting problems, after this method.

Useful tip

Talk to other parents about how they trained their children, and which method they would recommend.

Do it in days

Some parents choose a date, take their child's daytime nappies off and stay at home until the child uses the potty. If you have time, and can suspend normal life for a while, this method may suit you. The steps to follow are on the right. This method only works if you try it at the right time for your child. If you do, it may well work, but, if not, you will both have a miserable, negative, few days and probably have to give up and face doing it all again. Only attempt this method if you feel your child is already showing signs of being ready to be trained (see page 20).

No one can force a child to use the potty. It's best if they are willing, and ready, to do so.

Intensive method

1. Buy a supply of pants and comfortable clothing for your child. Cancel everything for the next few days. Get mops, cloths and disinfectant ready.

2. Explain what will happen, then take your child's nappy off. Take them to sit on the potty very regularly, for several minutes at a time.

3. Make sure your child drinks plenty of fluids, such as diluted fruit juice, to make them need to wee often. Keep putting them on the potty.

4. Keep reinforcing the message that your child must wee and poo in the potty. Praise successes and deal with accidents calmly.

Let them decide

Many experts suggest waiting for a child to indicate that they want to use the potty or toilet rather than nappies and then helping them make the transition into pants. Research shows that children today are being trained later, and bigger, more absorbent, nappies make it easier to keep a child in nappies for longer. In fact, some nappies are so efficient that children may not feel uncomfortable in a wet or dirty nappy and therefore may not learn to understand their body's signals. If your child is showing signs of being ready to be potty-trained, don't ignore them. It's vital to aim to balance your needs and your child's needs.

It can be embarrassing for a child to be in nappies longer than any of their playmates.

Special needs

Potty-training children with special needs is, in many cases, just like training any other child. There is no guaranteed method, each child makes different demands, and you need plenty of patience. There is also a huge range of different needs included in the term 'special needs', as parents will be aware. This page can only give a very basic overview of things that might be helpful.

Getting advice

It is a good idea to talk to the health professional who supports you and your child about any specific concerns you may have about potty-training before you begin. Some children with particular needs will learn to understand and control their body's toileting behaviour with ease, whereas others will take longer and need more help from their parents and carers.

Professionals are trained to advise on this. There are also books and websites with detailed information about particular special needs. You will find a list of them on the Usborne Quicklinks Website (see opposite page). On the left are three things it might be helpful for you to bear in mind before you begin potty-training a child with special needs.

Don't hesitate to ask for professional help if you need it.

Three tips

• Aim to focus not on your child's age in months and years, but on their physical and emotional readiness to be trained.

• Look out for the signs of readiness to start being trained listed on page 20. Your child must be ready to come out of nappies to master the toileting skills they need next.

• Remember that your child not only has to understand what their body needs to do, but also be able to get to (or show that they want to get to) the potty or toilet in time to do it.

Some children take longer than others to learn what a potty is for.

What not to do

Potty-training a small child is not always easy and parents often make the same mistakes. On the right are three of the most common. If you do them too, you are not alone, but be aware that they will only make a bad situation worse.

It's not always easy to stay cheerful during potty-training, but try not to let it spoil the time you spend with your child.

Internet links

The internet is a good source of information for parents and carers. At the Usborne Quicklinks Website there are links to lots of websites you may find useful and other things you can download. To visit the sites, go to **www.usborne-quicklinks.com** and type the keywords 'potty training'. Here are some of the things you can do via Usborne Quicklinks:

• *Print out the potty training chart from pages 55 to 57 of this book.*

• *Download reward charts and achievement certificates to help motivate your toddler.*

• *Watch video clips with lots of extra advice and tips on potty training your child.*

• *Print out colouring pages and song sheets to help make potty training a positive experience.*

There is a huge amount of advice about potty-training on the internet (but only some of it may be useful).

Internet safety

The websites recommended in Usborne Quicklinks are regularly reviewed. However the content of a website may change at any time and Usborne Publishing is not responsible for the content or availability of websites other than its own.

Index

With thanks to...

Bethan, Rhiannon and Mari;
Staff, parents and children at Cannons Health Club Nursery, Surbiton,
and Finley Mason;
Sam Taplin for proofreading;
Jessica Greenwell for indexing and website research;
Claire Masset for additional picture research.

Photo credits:

The publishers are grateful to the following for permission to reproduce material:

p9 © Luca DiCecco/Alamy; p15 © Bubbles Photolibrary/Alamy;
p18 © Jose Luis Pelaez, Inc./Corbis; p21 © Steve Prezant/Corbis;
p49 © Digital Vision/Alamy; p50 © Peter Dazeley/Alamy;
p54 © Picture Partners/Alamy

Additional illustrations: Dubravka Kolanovic

Digital imaging: Keith Furnival